PETER S. LINNEY

WORLD-FAMOUS AUTOMOBILE PHOTOGRAPHER

PRESENTS

picture
perfect

THE BEST OF AMERICA'S CUSTOM CARS

Peter S. Linney
Picture Perfect
The Best of America's Custom Cars

Whitman
Publishing, LLC
PUBLISHING SINCE 1934
www.whitman.com
© 2012 Whitman Publishing, LLC

Correspondence concerning this book may be directed to the publisher, at the address above.

ISBN: 0794837964
Printed and assembled in the United States of America.

To view other products from Whitman Publishing, please visit Whitman.com.

TABLE OF CONTENTS

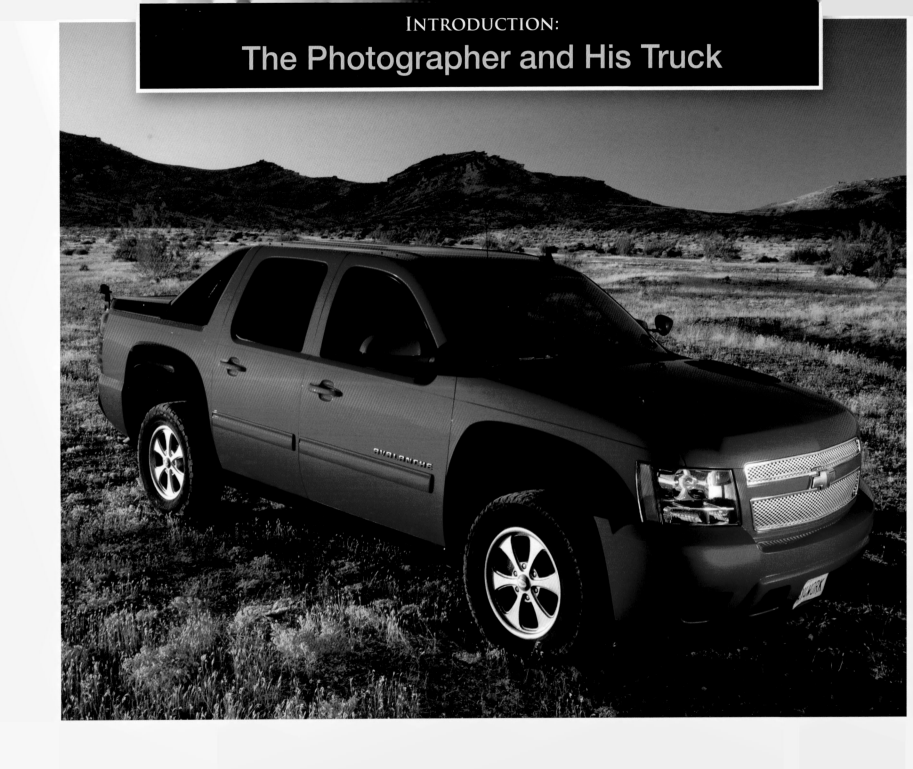

As an automobile photographer, I have learned that planning and focus is essential for a good photo shoot.

The planning consists of finding the perfect collectible car, ...g up the right sunset time with the owner at a location that is reasonably ... to where he lives, and making sure we both arrive there at least two ...s before sunset, or three hours if also shooting video.

...Once I get to a shoot, its success depends on the equipment I need for ... an endeavor. Some car photographers use natural three-fourths front-...ear angles to the sun to light the car, and it can look good. But it depends ...much on what your background is, and since I do most of my shoots on ...West Coast and like to see the ocean and beach behind my cars, I have big ...shiny boards with me to use as reflectors. I have six of them stacked on a ...in the back of my 2011 Chevy Avalanche.

...As an automotive journalist, I have the opportunity to drive and shoot ...y cars, but it takes sophisticated equipment that I keep in the truck. ...Avalanche holds all my equipment in a big drawer located under the ...ctors. I also have a big inverter inside that gives me all the light I need on ...n-setting location, where I put light inside the car and on the nose of the ...when I use the glow as my natural lighting source.

I have a number of camera mounts on the front and back of my truck ... corresponding monitors inside the cabin. So when you see a road-speed ... in this book, I had my Nikon camera on the back of the truck pointing at th... following me. I used a remote to trigger the camera while watching the i... on the monitor inside. To get the following car in the right spot, I talked wit... car owner on the Bluetooth in our vehicles. Because this system works, ... meet a car owner alone, and I never work with assistants, as it costs m... and takes more arranging — and it's my way of keeping the shoot in priv...

Bottom line is that you do need good equipment. I have the best N... camera and lenses, and I have been able to use them on my big feature... video as well. The Avalanche works superbly in both fields, and I unders... why it has received the "Best Truck" award from Consumer Union three y... in a row. We can all improvise, but for consistent high quality that ever... asks for these days, you must have professional equipment.

For more details on my vehicle and my photo shoots, please visi... website at www.autofocus.net.

1932 FORD ROADSTER

One of the things I discovered when I started to take photos of custom cars in the United States was that about 99 percent of the car owners were always the nicest people you would ever meet. And Jerry and Maureen Magnuson from Ventura, California, were no exception.

I had seen their 1932 Ford Roadster at the big car show in Pomona where it won the "most beautiful" award, and it moved to the top of my list of cars to photograph after that show.

My old friend and the best car designer in America, Chip Foose, built the car, which was a steel Murdoc replica of a 1932 Ford Roadster. The body was made from steel, and a fiberglass chassis made by Jerry Kugel from Kugel Komponents. Because of its incredible detail, it took six years to create this masterpiece!

The back wheels are 20 inches and fronts 17 inches to give it that special Roadster look, all on Pirelli tires, as this is a car built to go fast. The powerplant is a LS1 engine built by Kenny Dutweiller at about 348 horsepower, with a Magna Charger supercharger — a natural pick, as Jerry owns the company!

The paint came from BASF, and the two-tone paint scheme by Chip Foose. The leather upholstery work was crafted by Jim Griffin in Bend, Oregon.

Jerry and his shop also had their hands and minds on many parts of the car, like the dash, and the Sony radio.

We met more than once to get all the photographs done, as both are "car guys" of the best kind, and we had so much fun working with them. I say "we" because I brought my two daughters, ages 5 and 10, to the shoots, and they became instant friends.

The immediate challenge when you meet people like Jerry and Maureen Magnuson is to match the quality of their work with mine, and it was such a good feeling when I saw them at a car show a little later and they told me that my photos were their very favorite — and I know there were some "heavy-hitter" photographers who have had this car in for extensive photo sessions.

The last time we talked, the Magnuson's were already buried in a new build project, I told them I was standing by with my camera ready to go.

1932 FORD ROADSTER

THE BEST OF AMERICA'S
CUSTOM CARS

1932 FORD ROADSTER

13

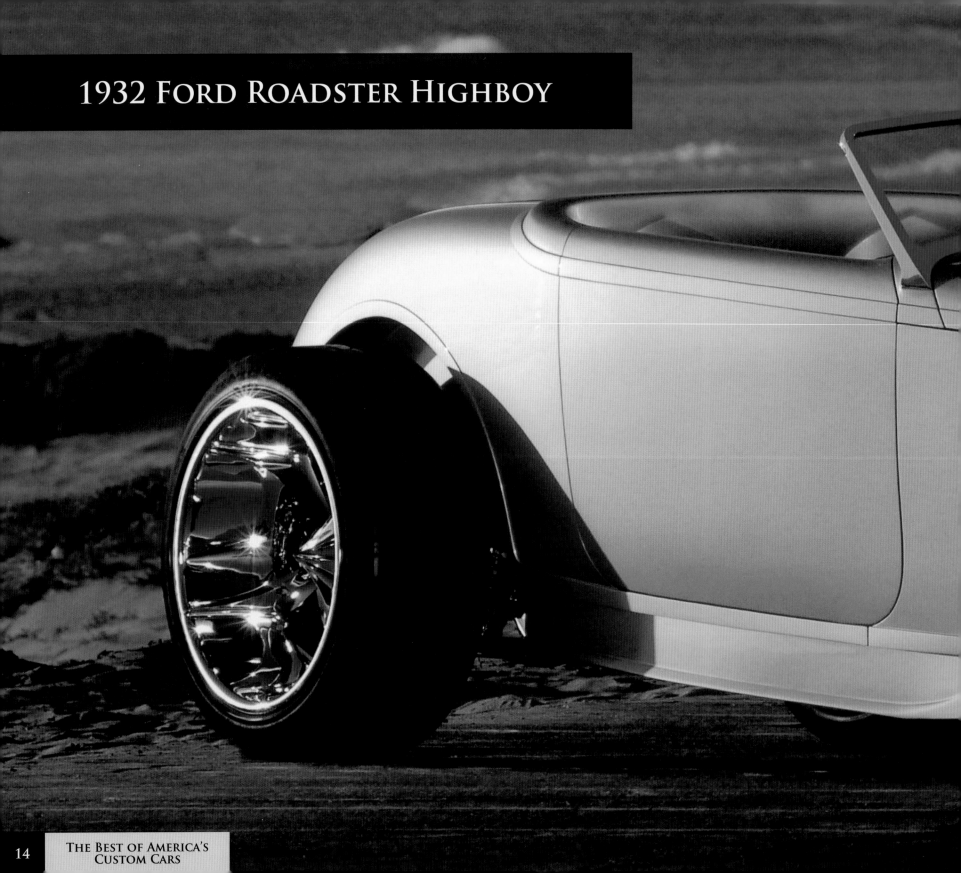

1932 Ford Roadster Highboy

The Best of America's
Custom Cars

When Ford introduced the Model B in 1932, it was a much updated version from a Model A. It came with a flathead V8, had about 65 horsepower and cost from $495 to $650.

This is where Rudy Necoechea's 1932 Ford Roadster Highboy started, but not much more than that. He took his ideas to Justin Padfield at Scott's HotRods and Customs in Ventura, California, and the entire project took over two years to finish.

Most of the body was built from scratch with custom tools. Compared to a standard '32, the body has been sectioned, doors lengthened and much, much more. What Rudy was aiming for was the "America's Most Beautiful Roadster" award, which is given at the Grand National Roadster Show in Pomona in January every year. It is a place where all serious hot-rodders flock to every year.

All body parts were basically handmade. Headwinds made the one-off designed headlights, and the "undisputed gold" color was made by BASF. Classic Instruments made all that was needed up on the dash, all very discreet and well placed. Boyd Coddington made a custom steering wheel from a drawing made by Rudy.

All four wheels are a marvel of engineering ability. What appears to be a spindle-mount wheel is actually a reverse hub wheel with a hidden mount. Boyd Coddington himself designed these wheels along with Rudy, and were CNC'd from solid billet aluminum slugs. The rear wheels are 22x12, and the front 20x7 and they sit on a custom front suspension made by Scott's Hot Rods. Wilwood Brakes made the four-piston 13-inch rear rotor and the six-piston 14-inch front rotor setups.

This is not a Sunday beach cruiser. It is 100 percent a trailer queen that comes with a professional crew. I am so glad we all came early on a pretty winter afternoon on Westward Beach in Malibu — just a dog walker and us. What a dream location to meet such a creative person as Rudy with his custom-made car. Rudy was probably the most perfectionist car owner I ever met. His crew was always making sure there was not a speck of dust on the car. The wheels were cleaned inside and out, and tire black was applied liberally. Every time we moved the car, the wheels were jacked up so that the wheel hubs could be properly positioned before I started shooting again.

But Rudy does know when he meets another creative person, and we both appreciated each other's craft very much. I had a very good time taking photos way past sunset on this most photographed beach in the world. And Rudy was there with the prize winner: "America's Most Beautiful Roadster" of 2008!

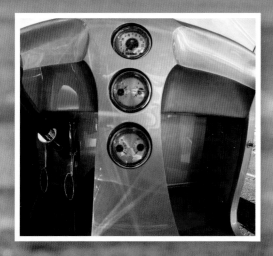

THE BEST OF AMERICA'S CUSTOM CARS

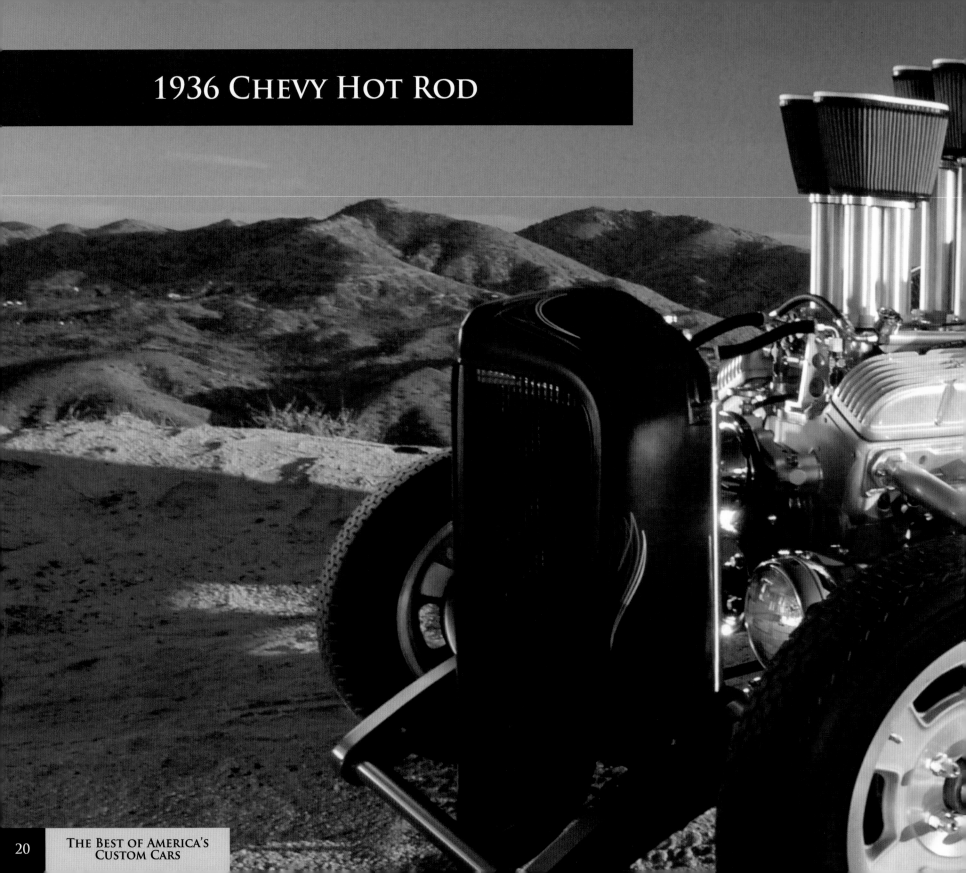

1936 Chevy Hot Rod

The Best of America's
Custom Cars

THE BEST OF AMERICA'S
CUSTOM CARS

Toby Stanford lives deep in the California desert in Yucca Valley where he runs a small but busy custom shop. Most of his clients are repeat customers who appreciate Toby's quality custom cars.

On the side, Toby builds personal cars with "not for sale" signs on them. It took a few years to get this 1936 Chevy just perfect. He started with a frame and a GM Performance four-bolt main engine with a 383 cubic-inch displacement. It was built with high-end polished aluminum parts, like heads by Edelbrock and a Hillborn intake manifold. He also has a vintage Hillborn injection system. Custom-built zoomie headers create a free exhaust straight from the engine.

There is a fine balance between the best-looking and the best-performing parts on a car and engine like this, but Toby has been in the business a long time and knows what works. A good example is the engine turned pattern on the firewall and dash. The radiator cover was also custom '36 Ford, and the louvered bed sides were all custom by his shop. Inside the car he has an all-leather bench seat made by local Ron Magnus. Stewart Warner made all the Silver Wing Gauges, again with that custom look Toby is so good at.

A Muncie M20 four-speed transmission coupled with a GM 12-bolt posi rear end with 31 spline Moser axels makes this hot rod truck a great driver. He has old-style 4x15 forged Vaughn wheels on the front and 11.5x17 on the back. This is not Toby's everyday ride but it is not gathering dust in his garage either. It is important to have some fun and, of course, it represents his work whenever he drives it to a show. Both novice and veteran guys can see that this is a professional's work.

THE BEST OF AMERICA'S
CUSTOM CARS

1936 Ford Roadster

1936 FORD ROADSTER

Ken Reister is definitely a car guy, but with a very high standard and aim in the world of custom cars.

I knew at once when I saw his beautiful car that this was one I had to get in front of with my camera. Ken is a very outgoing guy who liked my style, and we had a lot of fun in the California sunset photographing his custom car.

Here is the story Ken told me about the car:

"In 1999, at the Detroit Autorama, Chip Foose and I had dinner at a nearby restaurant. Over the course of conversation, we began talking about our dreams of building special cars. I described to Chip my favorite style of Street Rod and my idea to build one. His eyes brightened. He said, 'I've had an idea for a design like that for a long time,' and he began to draw on a napkin. The end result was great, and I got excited about the prospect of building a car like this.

"When Chip returned to California, I set a date to fly there and visit him. He drew more detailed pictures of his idea, and I got even more excited. A deal was struck to begin construction, and the car evolved from there. Over the years, it was great to see the smiles on people's faces as this special project took shape. Many of the craftsmen who worked on this car asked to be a part of the construction team.

"Without fail, all of the individuals involved put 100 percent of themselves and their talents into the job. It was amazing to watch some of the best craftsmen in the world motivated to produce their best work. Some of the work on this car was redone not by my request, but by their need to satisfy themselves that the end result was as good as it could possibly be.

I can't even begin to describe the feeling I had building this car. It was like my dream and Chip's vision became everyone's dream. I feel very special to own this car. My thanks and gratitude go out to Brian Fuller and all the guys at Foose Design, the guys at my shop (Dennis Graff and Trent Trimble), and all the craftsmen around the United States who were involved with the project. They created not only a work of art, but a piece of Street Rod history."

1936 FORD ROADSTER

THE BEST OF AMERICA'S
CUSTOM CARS

1936 CODDINGTON WHATTHEHAYE

THE BEST OF AMERICA'S
CUSTOM CARS

One of the first hot-rod builders I met and became friends with was Boyd Coddington. He and his chief designer Chip Foose would welcome me with open arms at their garage in Stanton, California, where I would shoot images of a car coming together before photographing it at a beach location.

The Whatthehaye was one such car, and it was one of the last Boyd made a few years before he passed away in 2008.

Boyd's garage boss Todd Emmons tells the story about the Whatthehaye:

"The Whatthehaye has lines from the French-built 1936 Delahaye, considered one of the most beautiful car designs in automotive history. After the Whatthehaye's design was finalized, Boyd's crew began working on the chassis using Art Morrison frame rails, with an independent front suspension and a Boyd Coddington Pro Ride independent rear suspension. Also bolted on were Boyd Coddington disc brakes and coil-over shocks.

"Once completed, the chassis was sent to Marcel's to hand-fabricate the body using sheets of steel; the removable hard top and deck lid were shaped using aluminum. Once Marcel finished shaping the body, it was delivered back to Boyd Coddington's garage, where it was pre-assembled, readying it for a DuPont silver-and-black paint scheme.

"Power is supplied by a Viper V-10 backed by a six-speed gearbox. A set of 18-inch one-off Boyd Coddington billet wheels were designed for the car, using Goodyear tires.

"After final assembly, the Whatthehaye was shipped to Gabe's for upholstery. The theme of simple elegance was carried throughout the car's interior, with black leather on the seats and door panels, and black carpet for the floor.

"To keep an eye on the V-10, Boyd Coddington gauges were installed in the steel dash. Another unusual aspect of this Coddington creation is the lack of any polished billet on the interior. Any billet, such as the Boyd Coddington steering wheel, shifter handle and foot pedals, were anodized black, making for a very clean, yet striking, interior.

"The Whatthehaye made its debut at the 2004 Barrett-Jackson Auction Gala in Scottsdale, Arizona, and took the crowd by surprise. Pictures cannot do this automobile justice; it requires viewing in person to fully appreciate its beauty."

1936 CODDINGTON
WHATTHEHAYE   35

THE BEST OF AMERICA'S
CUSTOM CARS

1936 CODDINGTON
WHATTHEHAYE

1937 PACKARD

THE BEST OF AMERICA'S
CUSTOM CARS

The 1937 Packard was a premier luxury car, even though not many of them were built. They introduced the first six-cylinder engine for the car, but it unfortunately arrived just in time for the 1938 recession, and there was not very much response to this change. The fact was it remained a toy for the rich who were not very brand loyal.

During World War II, Packard got caught up in war production, but they built the Merlin engine from Rolls Royce that powered the famous P-51 Mustang. After the war, they were in a very good economic position, but management was not knowledgeable on modern automobile production. Some say the old tooling was left out to rust during the war. So with a lack of materials after the war, they did not do very well.

But none of this mattered at all to Jim "Bones" Noteboom, the traditional custom car builder in Hemet, California. He knew of an original 1937 Packard sitting in a friend's shed for years, and after he bought it from his friend, it sat in Noteboom's garage for three more years while he was making up his mind about how to customize it. But after a while, Noteboom received some advice from Ken Ginning and Steve Stanford on what to do, and he worked for the next 18 months to make a real custom car out of the '37 Packard.

Noteboom put a 1955 Packard V8 under the hood, custom air cleaner and rocker covers, but left it pretty much stock — rebuilt with all modern parts, of course.

What often turns such a car into a treasure is a luxurious leather interior, which on Noteboom's car was done by DeLuxe Auto Interiors in Rosamond, California. But the real work is in the metal, such as cutting the hood 2 inches up front, sectioning the car 3 1/2 inches in the front, and lowering the front and back fenders. The running boards were handmade, along with all the chrome by Lil Louie. Colorado Custom provided the 1985 Mustang steering wheel, and he used Mercedes wool carpets. Ken Ginning's Body Shop did all the metal work. He used Wheel Smith Spokes and Coker radial tires. Air Ride Technology took care of the smooth road feel and handling. Noteboom painted the car in a deep green from House of Kolor.

Anyone who has seen the car would agree that the Packard boys would still be around today if Noteboom had been their design boss.

There is a sad footnote to this story. When Noteboom was on his way to a big show in Sacramento, the brakes on his trailer locked up, and the whole rig and car burned to the ground before he could get the fire out. Enjoy these photos, as they are the last visuals you will likely see of this fine automobile.

THE BEST OF AMERICA'S
CUSTOM CARS

1937 Coddington Smoothster

THE BEST OF AMERICA'S
CUSTOM CARS

Like so many projects in the hot rod industry, the Smoothster saw its conception in a different garage. It was Larry Erickson (of ZZ Top's CadZZilla fame) and his sheet-metal man Craig Naff who teamed up again for something with an equally high standard — and from scratch!

They would use the inspiration from a 1937 Cabriolet, a General Motors frame, a 1992 Corvette engine, and Corvette front and rear suspension. A wooden shell was made to get the right proportions, and everything was hand-fabricated the old-fashioned way. But some time later, they ran out of energy to do all this, so Boyd Coddington — with his very talented designer, Chip Foose — took over.

Team Coddington retained the overall shape of the original Erickson-Naff car that they were calling "Thirty Something." The original wheels were 14 inches, but Boyd changed that to 16 inches up front and 18 inches in the back. All wheels were made from big blocks of aluminum. The car was low, and a lot of work and care went into fabricating the exhaust system, with it running under the running boards. They were also looking for a very comfortable driving position, paying much attention to seats and pedals.

The art deco nose was handmade by George Gould and Chip Foose at Boyd's shop — one piece at the time. How much art and how much mechanical skill was needed? These are made by big stamping machines with "normal" cars, but on this car, they made it all by hand and ended up with an equally tight fit. I admire such mechanical and creative brains. After years of construction, I told them I would do an equally great job photographing the car.

Boyd was looking for a true roadster and not a trailer queen. To prove this, he and famous hot rod writer Gray Baskerville drove the car to Lincoln, Nebraska, on that year's Rod & Customs Americruise.

We have lost those two heavyweights in the hot rod industry, as Gray passed away in 2002, and Boyd in 2008. Gray always had time for me when I was visiting his Petersen Publishing office. I was a very junior photographer, and he gave a lot of advice and pointers to me. Boyd's wife, Jo, keeps his memory alive in social media. Boyd always asked me what he could do for me at his Stanton shop, where his doors were open for me to walk anyplace. It is an honor to publish several of his cars in this book.

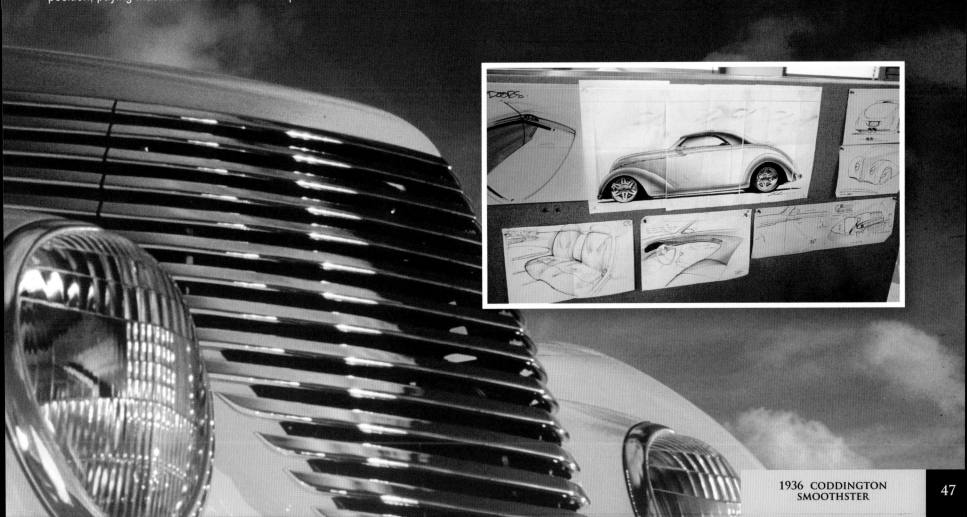

THE BEST OF AMERICA'S
CUSTOM CARS

1936 CODDINGTON
SMOOTHSTER

49

1949 Ford Hot Rod

51 Ford Hot Rod   51

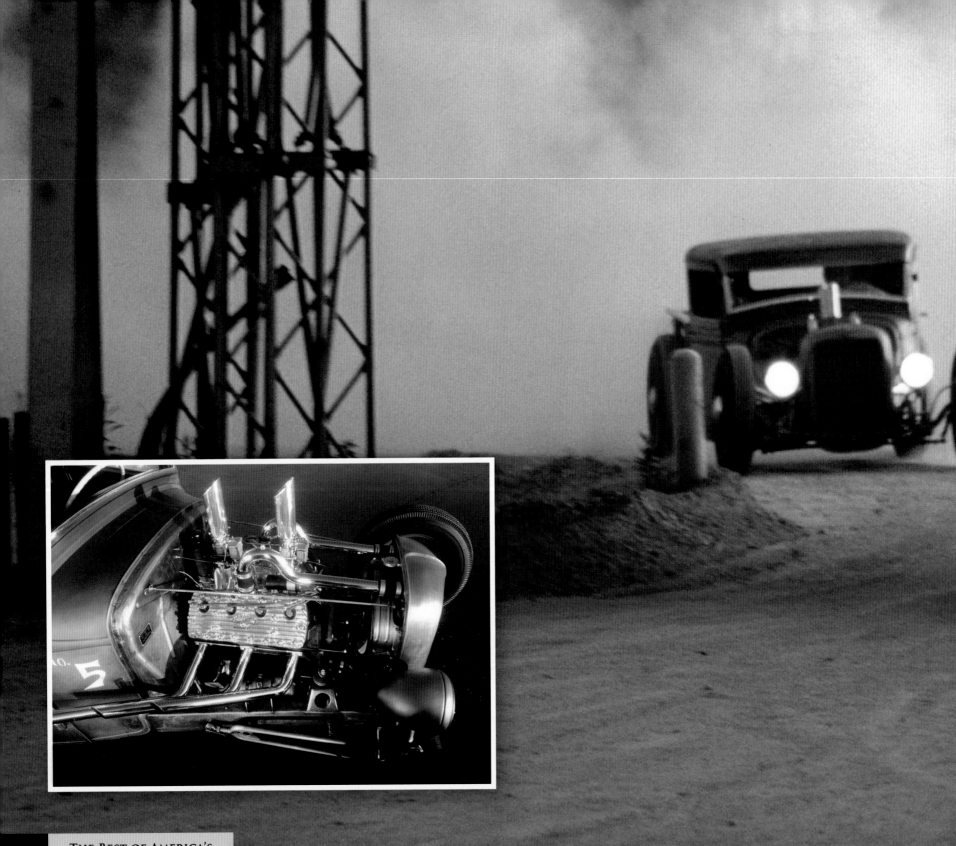

Jimmy Shine works at the very famous So-Cal Speed Shop in Pomona, California. Started by Alex Xydias just after his 1946 discharge from the U.S. Army Air Corps, it has a very long tradition in hot rod circles on the West Coast.

Jimmy is a welder and fabricator who fit right in at So-Cal, which had a long list of deep-pocket customers who saw the industry the same way as they did. As so often happens, guys like Jimmy have their own projects in the back of their mind. He bought the pieces for his project almost seven years earlier, and then chopped, channeled, narrowed, raked and boxed the 1949 Ford pickup with a 175-horsepower flathead. It started to look very good in a corner of the shop. He then added some good-looking twin Strombergs on the top of the engine and a set of zoomie headers.

We had a ton of fun out on location when I photographed the car, but Jimmy can tell the story much better than me:

"I had the idea for a Ford pickup in my head for probably 15 years. It started to come together when I bought it for $500 from a friend who found it in a sand wash 25 years earlier. It only consisted of half the doors, no floor, no firewall, no bed and no drive train — the bare essentials of a hot rod beginning. I worked at So-Cal Speed Shop, still do, and with the help and advice from some of the best minds in the industry, and combined with working after hours, the rod started to take shape."

Jimmy used a 1949 Ford flathead with an Edelbrock intake manifold. Air intake and many other parts was custom built by Jimmy, including the missing floor and firewall. The seats were from a 1952 J57 Aircraft and made of aluminum. Pulling it all was a 1939 Ford three-speed with a '37 tower shifter. The gas tank sits in the bed and once served as a hydraulic reservoir on a B-52 Bomber. The front wheels are 18 inches and the backs 16 inches, both with Firestone tires.

All in all, this is a hot rod anyone can see is built by a purist and enthusiast.

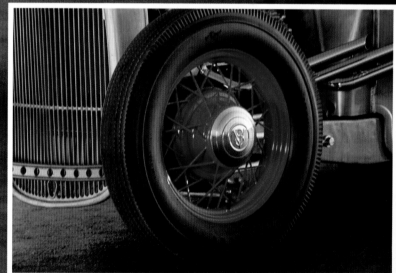

THE BEST OF AMERICA'S
CUSTOM CARS

Rick Dore and I have known each other for many years. It was an annual thing for me to drive from California to see him in Arizona before the summer became too hot. I was always photographing topnotch cars, and I enjoyed his creativity. I must admit I am a bit of a creativity groupie. People who can do stuff like Rick are very interesting to work with.

It is always my goal with anyone who I meet with a great custom car that I must do just as good work as they have, or better. I had a super opportunity on this project, as I was in his shop as the car he was using as a foundation for this build had just arrived from San Francisco as a two-door hardtop, and I took photos of it in its original look.

The next time I saw the car was at the annual Grand National Roadster Show in Pomona the following January, and it moved to the top of my list of cars to shoot. But no Arizona trip this time, as Carlsbad was now Rick's new home, and that is where we photographed this fantastic car.

I feel these are some my best color photographs, as they pop in the light that I like to use the most: "The Glow." Have you never seen "The Glow"? On a clear day, just look at where the sun just went down, it is a lot of clear light on a deep blue sky that colors any chrome on any car, and this Cadillac has a lot of chrome!

But, as usual, Rick did not follow the factory line on the chrome and bumpers. Yes, of course it is a 1950 Cadillac, but there are billets molded to a '55 Caddy bumper. And instead of the chrome headlight bezels, he Frenched the headlights, and also molded in two real nice air scoops on the side. The windshield was also custom, and he made it 2 inches lower. There are no door handles, and the stainless strip behind the door — so familiar on all 1950s Cadillacs — was replaced by five small bullets, and the whole side was given a more Eldorado-like look.

The seats are all leather, and the carpets are Mercedes done by Bob Devine. The blue color came from the House of Kolor and was painted by Art Wimsel and Caryl Hollenbeck. The car rides on Coker radials and Air Ride Technology. Rick used the original engine, which was easy to rebuild, and this is no trailer queen, as Rick made it to be a driver.

Rick builds a few cars a year, most for famous people like James Hetfield of Metallica and others. How much do they cost? Sorry, but if you ask, you cannot afford it.

THE BEST OF AMERICA'S
CUSTOM CARS

1951 MERCURY

THE BEST OF AMERICA'S
CUSTOM CARS

It did not take long after the first models came out for customizers' sharp eyes to hit the Mercury Eight. The engine was now a flathead V8 — a must have — and they used full instrumentation, and an eight-tube radio was an option. Sam Barris built the first "lead sled" from a Mercury Eight.

My good friend Rick Dore is a customizer who knows what to do with a Mercury Eight. Born in New York, Rick had a passion for all things automotive from a very early age. Influenced by the classic coachbuilders like Figoni & Falaschi, America's pioneering customizers, and the amazing concept vehicles dreamed up in that era, Rick has created an unmistakable style of his own. His early career was spent in Arizona, where he styled and built a large collection of top award-winning custom cars.

Rick and his friend Keith Dean took just six months to build this one. No flathead V8 here, as they used a Chevy 350 that produced some 300 horsepower, over double what the original produced — and remember, this is a "lead sled." Borla's stainless exhaust created the good sound. The top was chopped, the nose smoothed and corners were rounded. The hood has little scoops, and the headlights were Frenched. The bumper was all custom, with integrated bumper horns from a Cadillac.

The interior was finished in leather, with hand-built panels, armrests and seats. The carpet was standard Mercedes wool.

Colorado Custom provided 15x6 wheels with Coker wide whitewall radials. What was very new was that he took a complete 1980 General Motors chassis to ride on, and he added Air Ride by Grunion.

As usual, it went on the show circuit soon after it was done. I first saw the car at the SEMA Show in Las Vegas, and immediately made a deal to shoot it in Arizona. All of Rick's cars are made to be drivers, and we had a lot of fun that sunny afternoon outside Phoenix.

THE BEST OF AMERICA'S
CUSTOM CARS

1953 Cadillac Convertible

The Best of America's
Custom Cars

I found this car in a back yard in Hollywood in the mid-1980s. Then I restored the car so I could use it on my photo shoots.

I had an expert rebuild the engine, while I did the new seats, top and paint job. I bought wire wheels from Roadster Wheels in Los Angeles, as they make duplicate wheels for the Cadillac, and I used Coker whitewall radial tires.

Then I drove the car and put about 60,000 miles on it! The only maintenance I did was general service, although I installed a high-flow radiator to better manage LA's hot summers.

In 2002 I bought a Chevrolet Avalanche as my work truck and I left the car with a friend who did a lot of top engine work on it. Then after a few years of storage and a transmission rebuild, I stripped the chrome and stainless steel, and it was taken to a very good painter. Months later, it had a glass-finish paint job, and I took it to an old-fashioned upholstery man who made a new cloth top, and new all-leather seats. It took a long time, but it looked very good.

Then I drove the car to a friend who is a Cadillac expert. He and I worked on it every day for almost three months to get the car back to its factory original state. I have many new chrome and polished stainless steel parts. The windshield is new, and so is all the rubber. I have a new factory-looking wiring harness, but it was made with modern material so it does not crack. The fuse box is now under the hood and not under the dash, which was an impossible place to find it before. I also have two new outside mirrors, both with the correct date code.

I have driven the car about once a week after I had it tweaked so it runs real well in traffic or on the freeway. I had a leak around the transmission, so an old-fashioned transmission guy replaced all gaskets and seals, and also had a look inside. Most everything was 100 percent, but he found a few things to improve on.

This is an old car, but it is a very simple old car, and it never let me down when I was using it every week.

THE BEST OF AMERICA'S
CUSTOM CARS

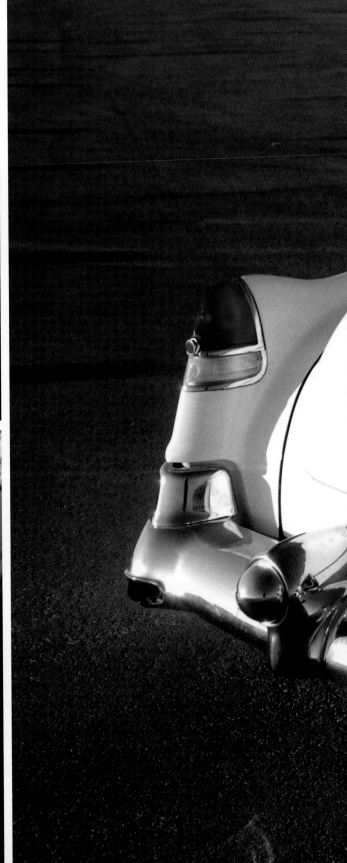

THE BEST OF AMERICA'S
CUSTOM CARS

1953 Studebaker

The Best of America's
Custom Cars

For this classic 1953 Studebaker, I will let car owner Leonard Knight from Glendora, California, tell his story:

"I've known Vince at J.V. Enterprises in Azusa, California, for about 10 to 12 years now. I met him by accident after buying a 1939 Ford that I wanted to make a restoration rod out of. I had rented a storage space and one day on my way over I noticed his shop. I stopped in to talk to him and ended up having him do all the work. In the subsequent years, he has modified that 1939 Ford three times. He built a 1932 Ford Roadster with a Viper motor that competed in the Grand National Roadster show, a 1934 Ford Coupe, and various other modifications to other cars.

"Being a horsepower and speed nut, I had always gone for straightline performance. However, after getting into amateur roadracing with the Viper Club, I found it was more fun to turn corners. I had always liked the 1953 Studebakers, and I especially like the hardtop models. I talked to Vince about some ideas I had, and he told me his ideas. We ended up going in the direction of a touring-type car but with a lot of horsepower.

"We decided on a direction, and the search started for the car. I looked at a number of cars and finally came across my 1953 Studebaker in Oakland. I made the deal over the phone and drove up with my trailer to pick it up. The car was being stored on the docks in Oakland under a tarp, but it actually ran. It looked quite good, so I loaded it up and drove home.

"Vince then started the disassembly, media blasting, etc. and we found that the car had been repaired with a lot of sheet metal screws, Uncle Henry's roofing sealer and patch pieces.

"For the next 26 months Vince worked his magic on the car, chopping 5 1/2 inches out of the top, tilting back the windshield, widening the rear fenders, and reshaping the doors and rockers. In order to make the car right, every panel had to be modified. He was able to take the chop from under the front window so that we could maintain full-sized front and rear windshields, which was no small feat.

"We wanted the car to be very fast but also very driveable. I normally like big cubic-inch motors with big injection systems or big blower systems, but after talking with Turnkey Engines they advised that I could get 1,000 horsepower out of a motor that drove in the city, like a stock 350 Chevy. This was the only way to go since I wanted to go around corners as well as in a straight line.

"Turnkey went to work building me an engine. Vince then determined that there was no way the stock or even reinforced stock frame would do what we wanted, so he constructed a new very strong custom frame. After putting the car together and getting the paint on it — which is both eye catching and subtle — we corner-weighted the car, and it came out nearly a 50/50 weight balance.

"I plan to autocross the car once I finish showing it. I believe in driving them. I have about 800 miles on the car now, even though my schedule has not allowed much time for driving. The car is solid, handles like a dream, and is as dependable as any new car. It will be hard for me to top this one!"

1953 Studebaker

THE BEST OF AMERICA'S
CUSTOM CARS

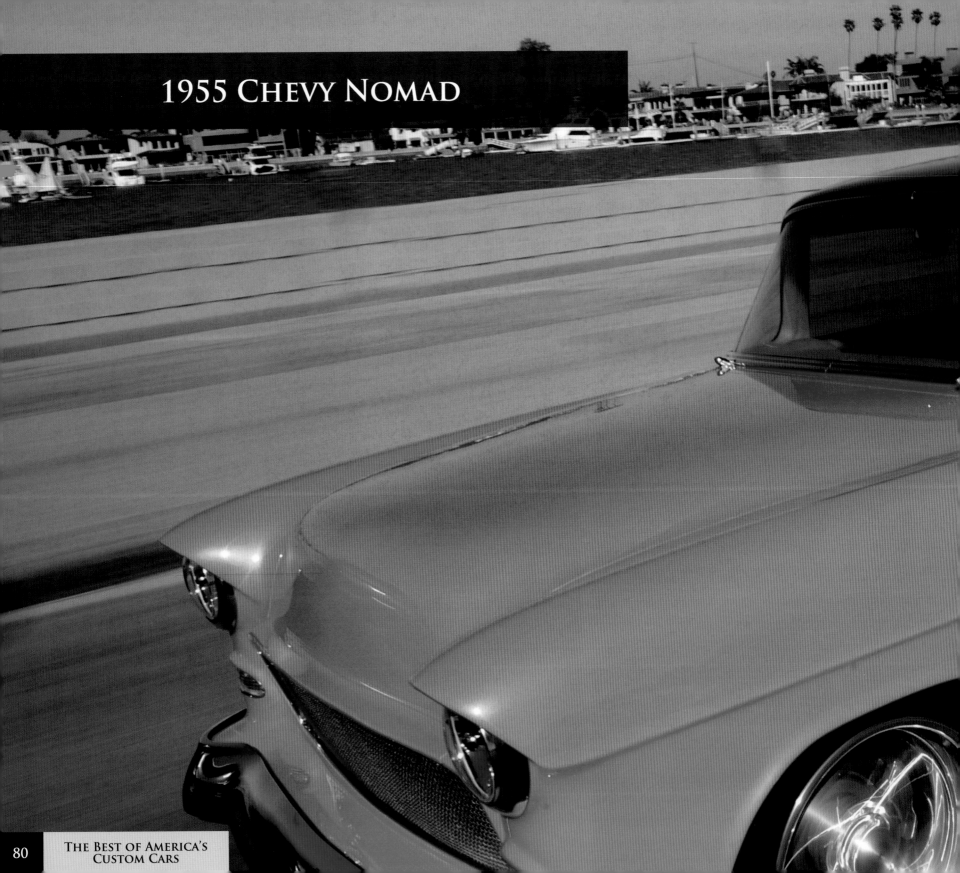

1955 Chevy Nomad

The Best of America's
Custom Cars

THE BEST OF AMERICA'S
CUSTOM CARS

Don Chambers from Long Beach, California, was already a veteran inside the custom car culture when he found a 1955 Chevy Nomad in Canada.

He drove a 1954 Chevy Cameo pickup when he was in high school and he kept driving it for years afterward. Then later when he was a police officer in Gardena, he drove a '68 lowered Buick Riviera. He often had a hard time coming down on the school kids in his district when they drove too fast or were doing late-night drag racing. He even decided an argument about who won as he and other cops were shutting down a race late one night on a dark industrial street. Chambers says it was more fun advising those young guys and their girlfriends on car safety and construction.

That was on his mind when he started the Nomad project after he retired in 2001 and had plenty of time on his hands. He is lucky everything was original on the Nomad, but he had a new frame and Camaro motor, and front and back suspension, sent in from the Roadster Shop in Illinois. He took the car apart, had it powder coated, had it assembled by Kugel in California, and then fitted with Wilwood brakes. They had the body lifted and finished underneath by the time the new chassis rolled in to a perfect fit.

The next stop was to wire some life into that low-mileage Camaro engine. It was an IROC 350 tuned port. Don and Frank at Ultimate Chassis did the wiring and the engine started up the very first time. Hooker headers and Flowmaster exhaust made the car sound great, and it gave Don renewed energy to tackle all the new body modifications, starting with lowering the roof 1 inch from the B pillar and back. The drip rails were cut smaller and molded. On the front, the peal was removed, holes filled and a front piece was fabricated. Same with the headlight bezels, which were made using the originals, clay and fiberglass. He also made the aluminum covers for the engine.

He gave it a Chevy 700R4 transmission, which along with the engine was pretty much stock, so all service and maintenance is kept to a minimum, and the car is a normal "everyday driver" — something that was the goal from the beginning — though a very pretty "everyday driver." The rear end is a 9-inch Ford limited-slip differential. The front and rear wheels are 18x8 from Budnik with Continental tires.

Chambers did not like the split back door, as it had a habit of rattling a lot and had two ugly hinges at the bottom. So he started to build a one-piece tailgate. He used the same top hinges that are nicely hidden, but added two 100-pound struts that hold the whole frame with the old window and bottom up without any problem. With this, the major construction was done, but he worked on some modified Cadillac bumpers. He had the car painted pearl orange, and the front seats came from Rich Santana, and the back ones built by Dave Galindo at House of Trim.

This is now a "modern" running car that Don drives almost every day while getting respect from his peers every time he takes it to a show or early morning meeting.

1955 Chevy Nomad

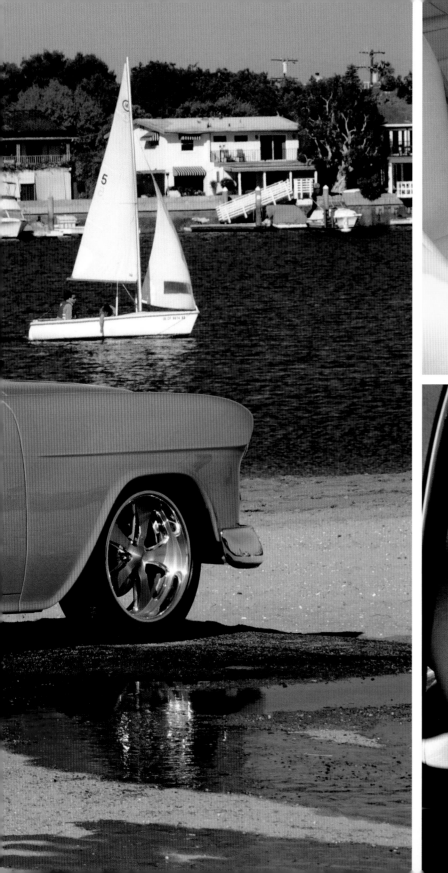

1956 Chevy Bel Air

The Best of America's
Custom Cars

THE BEST OF AMERICA'S
CUSTOM CARS

Most of you may think all great custom cars were built in the United States, but there is a universal love of these cars all over the world, and Scandinavia is no exception. They love all American cars, and when they restore them, only the very best parts are used.

Paal Skaalsvik is a Norwegian who loves customizing American cars. Skaalsvik's 1956 Chevy Bel Air is a "nice driver," and not just a show car. It had to be finished in time for the 50th anniversary for the '56 Chevrolet in 2006.

His goal for this car was to build a '56 Chevy with a classic look, but with the chassis built for 150 miles per hour. He also wanted to drive it for the next 20 years — including on long trips — without anything other than the required normal service. To reach this goal, Skaalsvik had to use only the best parts, and try to use as much as possible from a standard drive train.

In summer 2004, Skaalsvik's full-time job was taking up 10 to 12 hours a day, so to build a car like this in Norway near the sunlight-deprived Arctic Circle is not easy. During the last winter of working on the car, he was spending a minimum of 25 hours a week in his garage.

Skaalsvik did a lot of online research to get the best frame for this project. He chose Car Creations in California because of its preparation for original Chevrolet parts in a modified original frame. The body had been sitting in his garage for several years, and it was a nice one with a minimal amount of work needed.

He decided to not change anything outside except the parking lamps in front. Inside, the goal was to give it a smoother look. He also added a 2004 Corvette 350 LS1 engine, but everything around it was made to look as factory as possible.

The car has received many honors in Scandinavia, especially in Sweden, and because of this, it was invited to the biggest indoor show in Scandinavia in 2007. At that show, the owner of the Grand National Roadster Show saw Skaalsvik's car and invited it to his 2008 show in California. The "nice driver" was now a show car, but it had 8,500 miles on it before the Grand Nationals.

I met Skaalsvik and his car at the Pomona show. People in Los Angeles are so used to seeing very nice custom cars that they don't pay too much attention to them, but after hanging with Skaalsvik and his car for a few days, I saw instant attention wherever we stopped. In fact, I had to push a little for us to get to the El Mirage shooting location before the sun set.

Later, Skaalsvik took this car out and got proof that it was a wise investment: a few speeding tickets from the California Highway Patrol!

1956 CHEVY BEL AIR

1956 Ford Gasser

I have known Steve Carpenter from Northridge, California, for a long time. Both of us are owners of classic Cadillacs, and Galpin Auto Sports where he works in Van Nuys makes some of the best custom Ford Mustangs in the United States, and I photograph Mustangs for magazines. So when we meet, we talk cars like old pros all the time.

Steve explains how the 1956 Ford "Gasser" came about:

"We at Galpin Auto Sport wanted to let people know that we are more than the No. 1 Mustang shop, that we do all cars and hot rods, so we came up with an old-school 'gasser' that we can drive on the streets and at shows. Our team of guys all own and drive hot rods, and this was so much fun for them that they worked all hours to build this car in six months.

"We found the car in North Carolina. It was an old drag car that had seen better days. It needed it all — motor, transmission, rear end, full interior, gauges, etc. We also did not want the car to be perfect, because they were not that way. We made the car street-legal, fast and easy to drive, and still kept the old gasser look and feel.

"First up, the semi-matte black was hand-painted so all the decals would show perfectly. They used a small-block Ford engine producing about 331 horsepower, and with a set of traditional Hooker heaters. The seats were re-upholstered from a Dodge motor home, and the roll cage was placed over those.

"Part of the look is the rear axle, a 9-inch 31 spline 411 posi traction, and a 411 drive ratio. Bolted to it are MT 12.5x15 ET street drags. The distinct front end is a '70 Ford Ecoline straight axle, and it gives the car its typical front list, with a round aluminum tank over that."

This is not your average morning commuter car, but a vehicle full of fun that gets a lot of looks wherever it goes.

THE BEST OF AMERICA'S CUSTOM CARS

1956 FORD GASSER

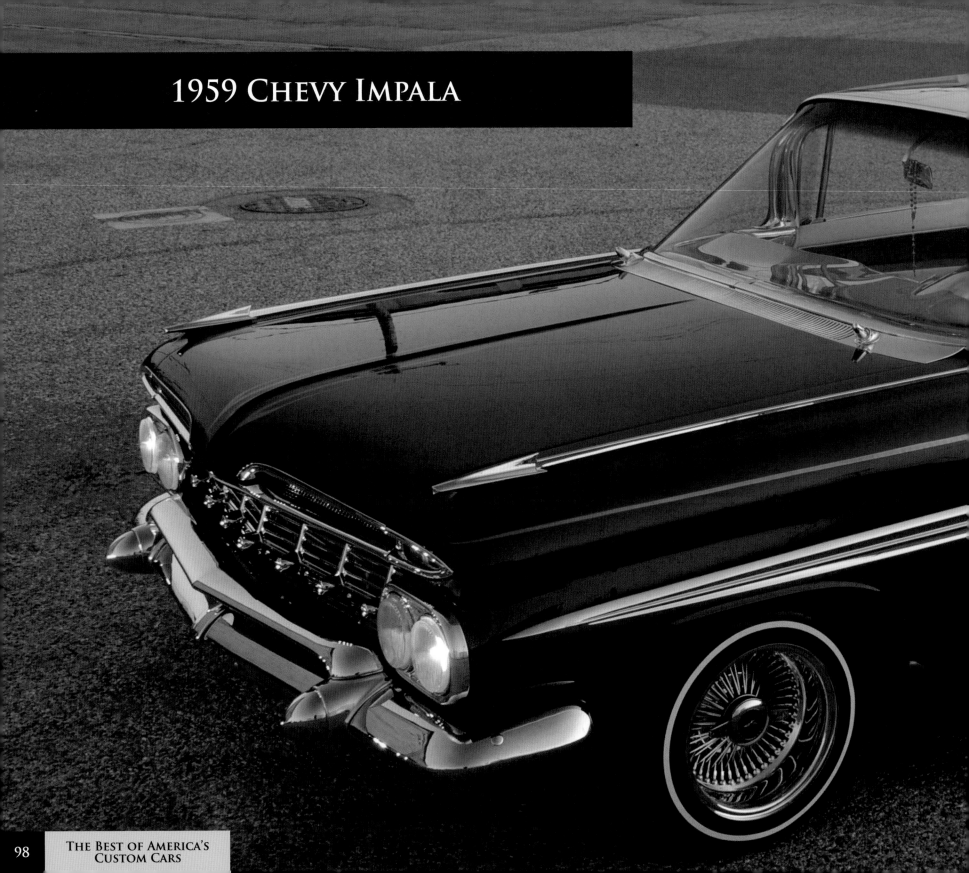

1959 CHEVY IMPALA

THE BEST OF AMERICA'S
CUSTOM CARS

I met Agostino Onorato at a big car show in Los Angeles that had many very nice cars, but his 1959 Chevy Impala stood out from the crowd.

It had a very high quality and the lowrider pedigree with all the right stuff on it for the look and performance. As part of the high quality, he had the body painted "kandy kobalt blue" at the House of Kolor, with added silver for balance with all the chrome. It also helped that Agostino's nephews, Frankie and Anthony Onorato, own Five-Star Detail Products, and know what it takes to max up the shine on a car.

The Impala has a 1959 Chevy engine with a few modifications, such as balancing, better crank and rods, and bigger pistons with an Edelbrock intake manifold. Headman headers connect to Magnaflow mufflers for the custom sound that's so important on these cars. On the body, the hood is stock, but the doors are "shaved," meaning no door handles. Both bumpers are stock, but on back you have the famous Continental kit. On the front and back are 88-spoke Daytona wire wheels with Cooper Trendsetter tires.

Henry's Custom Upholstery in Azusa did the entire interior in Italian leather and suede headliner. Dakota Digital took care of all instrument information, and Alpine supplied the radio. There is a lot of chrome work on a car like this, and all that was done by Greg Cox at Artistic Silver Plating in Long Beach.

It took Agostino seven years from start to finish, and as so often happens, he had a lot of help from family like Frankie and Anthony, and from professionals like Manuel Rojas on the suspension and Steve Deman on the body and paint work.

"I bought the car from a friend of mine who had owned it for several years," said Agostino. "He always maintained and kept the car in excellent shape. One day he had mentioned to me that he wanted sell it, so I couldn't resist, and I bought it from him. The car was originally black from the factory and still looked like it did when it rolled off the assembly line. After a few months of owning it and driving it, I decided to tear the car down completely and give it a custom facelift. Like I mentioned, the car was pristine, but I wanted to add my personal touches to the car and my taste to it. So after the longest seven years of my life, the car turned out to be what it is now — from mild to wild, from good to better. I'm proud to present to you my car, '59 Times.'"

THE BEST OF AMERICA'S
CUSTOM CARS

1959 Chevy Impala

Sean Cassar is the private-collector type I love to meet. They have such passion for their cars, and they build them the very best, and with pride.

Cassar's pride is a 1959 Chevy Impala two-door hardtop. He bought this car about three years ago from the original owner, but it did not quite look like it does now. In fact, he probably should have taken it directly to the junkyard! The car lived its whole life in Colorado before coming to California for its new look. Although the vehicle was not a Cali car, it was pretty solid but had some rust in the notorious spots for a '59.

This Impala is equipped with a LS1 motor package, 4L60E transmission and a custom-built Currie 9-inch Ford rear end. The motor has CNC ported and polished high-flow heads, a custom ground cam, a ported and polished custom intake system, and many computer programming mods to the stock ECU. All motor accessories are Street and Performance. The motor is cooled by a custom aluminum cross-flow radiator and a huge electric fan by Dakota Digital.

The car was upgraded to include power steering and an Ididit tilt steering column that he painted to match. The suspension is all Air Ride Technologies, also utilizing their Strong A-Arm system. The wheels are 22-inch and 20-inch Billet Specialties, while the Baer brakes and calipers are mounted on 2-inch drop spindles. Cassar ended up using a Wildwood master cylinder on the car simply because he liked the look of it against the painted and smoothed custom firewall.

The interior was designed and built by Alan Wray at Conejo Upholstery in Thousand Oaks. The front seats are 1964 Impala SS buckets that they cut and lowered so they would not sit above the window line. The car has just over seven full hides of leather in it!

Electronics include all-electric windows (including vents), Home Link System and full-memory Air Ride Control. Auto Meter gauges were sunk into the original dash to give it an almost-stock look. The dash was smoothed and the original radio was deleted, as well as the original heat and vent controls. The Impala's audio system includes an in-dash Pioneer 7-inch monitor, 10 total speakers and Rockford Fosgate amps and subs. Switches have been nicely disguised in the center console, so nothing is visible unless you want to access it.

This car has a major history to it, as it was designed by Harley Earl, who was in charge of styling for General Motors. Earl got pretty shaken up after viewing the new crop of Chrysler products that were being released. They were fresh, long and striking, and they had fins — fantastic fins of monumental proportions! Upon seeing these cars, it is said that Earl had all the existing 1959 GM designs scrapped in preparation for all-new cars. The '59

Chevy was the last car Earl designed for GM before retiring, and his flamboyant style was very evident. The rear fins, rather than sticking straight up, were placed nearly parallel with the road and dropped into a "V" in the center. The taillights were redesigned as a sideways teardrop to flow with the drop of the fins. The paired headlights were a complete departure from the individual lights of the previous year. The design would return to individual lights for 1960 and continue on for many years. The headlights were moved to the grille rather than above it, a style queue that was common for the model year that slimmed the look of the front end.

We are lucky to have guys like Sean Cassar, who 50-some years later preserves American culture by iconic designers like Harley Earl.

1959 CHEVY IMPALA

THE BEST OF AMERICA'S
CUSTOM CARS

I knew Tempie Abate through her husband and "car guy" Rick. After I did my photo shoot of her very pretty 1961 Cadillac Coupe de Ville, she provided the great details that follow:

"My 1961 Cadillac Colorado Caddy was built by legendary customizer Rick Dore. This custom Caddy has been nosed, decked and completely shaved, rear bumpers Frenched, and the rear fins cut, stretched, sharpened and filled. The stainless side trim was removed, door handles and emblems shaved, and lower character line enhanced to make this custom creation look low, lean, clean and mean.

"Sitting on one-off Colorado Custom Julesburg wheels especially made for this car, you just have to see it to believe it. It has a rebuilt 390 engine with 325-horsepower V8 to factory specs, automatic transmission and full Air Ride Technologies suspension. It was painted by Lucky 7 Customs' Marcos Garcia, featuring a House of Kolor custom mix of candy orange laid over a gold base with a custom mix of metal flake flames and pin stripping along the sides, hood and interior dash.

"The custom interior features fawn leather quad bucket seats, front to rear center console and 3D neo-classic headliner all hand built by Bob Divine. A Colorado Custom steering wheel finishes off the interior look, and it's way too cool. Now add a body-thumping, heart-pumping, full-custom 1,000-watt sound system with CD, Arc Audio 5150 amp with a 12-inch subwoofer and components, and you are good to cruise anywhere — not just in style, but way over the top.

"I, being an absolute classic car fanatic — not unlike many of my male counterparts — am always perusing the magazines, websites and car shows always looking for that next 'fix,' that next 'I gotta have it' car. When you go past that point of no return and it's suddenly yours, Eureka! Well that's what happened to me with this 1961 custom Cadillac.

"I saw this amazing custom car on the Internet several years ago and followed it for a couple years as it popped up here and there for sale, on and off different sites, and at different auction houses. Yep, every time I saw her, I drooled, and thought 'maybe,' 'someday' and 'only in my dreams.' Then one day it happened. I called a new owner of this car and he said he had to pay for his restaurant and could not keep her. I made him an offer, and after two years, in less than two minutes she was mine! I was awestruck, and instantly paralyzed at the same time, as I thought how I was going to justify to my husband what came over me and what would be arriving at our home in the next 30 days.

"When she rolled off the truck at our front door, site unseen, I was as smitten as a school teen on her first date. I spent the usual small fortune and many hours making her perfectly road worthy, as many new owners do, and have spent the last few years fully enjoying showing her off on the West Coast.

"She isn't my first and won't be my last, but she is definitely my favorite — at least for now. As for my husband, I bought him a custom Harley, which seemed to move the spotlight over just enough. You know what I mean, right guys?"

THE BEST OF AMERICA'S
CUSTOM CARS

1970 Dodge Charger

THE BEST OF AMERICA'S
CUSTOM CARS

THE BEST OF AMERICA'S
CUSTOM CARS

The 1970 Dodge Charger continued to use the same body as in the previous year, but it received a few minor trim changes. It featured a new loop bumper, new front fenders and concealed headlights.

This car came about because dealers were looking to compete with Ford's and Chevy's muscle cars. The 1970 Charger's very exotic look did help for a while, and its 440 Six Pack 390-horsepower engine also helped. Then all its NASCAR wins gave it a muscle-car pedigree.

Car builder Steve Strope from Pure Vision was a hired hand in rebuilding and styling this 1970 Charger for Petrol Advertising in Burbank, California. Pure Vision in Simi Valley was the perfect place for restoring and redesigning this car, and that included rear wheel tubs that were widened to accommodate Pirelli 345 tires and rear taillights that were changed to a 1968 panel.

On the front bumper, a 1/4-inch piece of metal was added to the outer edge of the bumper to eliminate the bumper-to-body gap. The grille was restored and painted all black.

"My customer wanted black, and I chose the stripe design," says Steve. "The stripe is taken from a Ferrari Tour de France race car paint scheme. That is also why I chose the '68 round taillights, because they are Ferrari-like.

"The seats are 1970 high-back buckets, custom foam and handmade covers to emulate Ferrari stitch pattern. This is very much a street machine, and it announces itself at least a block away!"

Steve explains how the car came together.

"The deadline for this car would be set for the 2006 SEMA event in Las Vegas, and a 1970 Dodge Charger would be vehicle of choice. Wanting to tap into the rich Mopar history, the iconic B-Body would be an ideal machine to exhibit both Petrol's interests and Pure Vision's craftsmanship.

"With no time to spare, the Charger was stripped down to a rolling chassis and media blasted. Once clean, the body was sent to Gold Coast Custom Inc., where the wheel tubs were opened to accept the larger rolling stock and sub-frame connectors to keep the Unitbody from twisting under the intended torque to come.

"Some tweaks were made to the '70 at an early stage that would stand out once the build was complete. The rear valance was pulled and replaced with that of a '68, eliminating the long, horizontal taillights and replacing them with the first year of the second generation Charger's thruster-like round tail lamps. The dash frame was pulled from the interior and exchanged with a modified and trimmed '71 Charger dash. At the close of its sojourn at Gold Coast, the body was meticulously prepped and straightened all to be finally coated in several layers of inky black paint before a vibrant orange stripe streaked back from the wrap-around front bumper to the tail."

And thus, Steve at Pure Vision and Petrol Advertising had brought another classic muscle car to life in California.

THE BEST OF AMERICA'S
CUSTOM CARS

THE BEST OF AMERICA'S CUSTOM CARS

I have known Patrick Nance's dad Daryl for many years, as he was a high-end Chevy restoration expert. When I saw Patrick's 1971 yellow Chevelle, I at once realized it was a high-quality build and I asked him if I could photograph it. Here is the story about Patrick's car in his own words:

"My Chevelle was a daily driver for a neighbor, and I used to see the car every day. I didn't see the car for a long time and I learned that the previous owner completely disassembled the car to restore it, but lost interest and started parting the car out. The car was incomplete and looked bad. I knew that the car had potential, so I bought it on the cheap and I developed a plan to turn the car into a cool, modern resto-mod Chevelle. Like many projects, it grew from a simple build to what you now see as an over-the-top "A" body.

"I worked on the car for about two years to get it to its current condition. There are numerous custom features throughout. I was asked to bring the car to the 2008 SEMA show and displayed the car in the Custom Autosound Booth.

"This car is driven regularly in 'Surf City' — Huntington Beach, California. My Chevelle is fast and fun to drive. I have shown the car a few times and it has won several awards. I hope that others with project cars are inspired to use their creativity to build a cool car that otherwise may have wound up at the crusher.

"I want to thank my family — Darryl, Peggy and my brother Nick — for helping with the build of this car. I would also like to thank all the guys at D&P Classic Chevy, including Kevin, Craig, Mike and Alex for the help on the car. Many companies helped with the build by providing products or support on this project.

Thank you to all who helped with this special car.

THE BEST OF AMERICA'S
CUSTOM CARS

ABOUT THE AUTHOR

I saw my first real American car in the late 1950s. I was walking a country road in mid-Norway where I grew up. It was a Chevy Impala with the big horizontal fins. If I had seen a UFO up close or that car, my reaction would have been the same. I was hooked, and I started reading up on anything I could find about American cars.

Luckily, American cars had, and still do have, a huge following in Norway and Sweden, and years later, I was able to photograph some of them. Back then on my photo shoots, I rented Jeeps that were not well maintained. But then in the mid-70s I bought my first Chevy 4x4 Blazer, and I had a blast driving and photographing it in Norway, Iceland and across the Sahara with a girlfriend. Camping all the way, it never let us down, and *Fourwheeler* magazine bought my first story about that trip.

But it was when I moved to the United States for AFI film school in early 1980s that I started shooting seriously for magazines. First were Norwegian and European publications, but I used the lighting techniques I had learned working on films, and soon U.S. magazines took notice, and magazines like *Truckin* and *Muscle Mustang* began using my stuff on a regular basis.

What I have discovered in this business is that all the people who own classics or build custom cars are super nice and very easy to work with — and they just love seeing pretty photos of these cars they had worked so hard on.

I grew up in nature, so light came quite natural to me. From there, I developed my way of using an inverter in my photo truck to light the nose of the car I am shooting, and a special rig to light the interior of the car just after the sun sets. It creates a very clean and natural look that became very popular. It's easy to do if you have a day in a studio, but not so easy when you have 10 to 15 minutes after the sun sets and you are using "The Glow."

People from different parts of the world have told me I "paint with light" and I very much agree. I also simply love what I do, and the hundreds and hundreds of cars I have photographed over 20 years now pass by as a happy blur!

— Peter S. Linney

ACKNOWLEDGEMENTS

I must, of course, thank my mom in Norway who supported me when I decided to become a photographer, and wherever I was in the world. I must also thank Margaret, my photo school teacher who taught me the value of using polarizing filters, which are so essential when you shoot cars.

I would like to thank very much the editors of *Car* magazine in London who gave me my first assignment, photographing the first Morgan + 8. It started a lifelong friendship with the Morgan family, and special treatment at buying three Morgan + 8s, from when I was 20 to when I was 30. So much fun and so many pretty photos.

It was when I moved to Los Angeles for film school and learned new ways of lighting when the real fun started, so thank you AFI.

Thanks also to: Mike Anson, who gave me the first pages in *Fourwheeler* magazine; Tom Vogele, editor at *Streetrodder* magazine; Hoyt Wandenberg at *Sport Truck* magazine; Kevin Wilson at *Truckin*, Terje Aasen, the editor of *Amcar* magazine in Norway who always supported me; and lately, Jim Campisano and Evan Smith, editors of *Muscle Mustang* and *SuperChevy*.

But the people who I am most thankful to are the men and women owners/builders of all the cars I have photographed — too many names to name here, but they know who they are. Without their time and enthusiasm, I would not have succeeded at what I do. They are a super-nice bunch of people who I could share my love for cars with.